A Bear with Electric Hair

Jaap Tuinman

CONSULTANTS
Sharon Anderson
Elaine Baker
Maxine Bone
Jill Hamilton
Diana Hill
Orysia Hull
Sandy Johnstone
Moira Juliebö
Beverley Kula
Helen Langford
Mary Neeley
Carol Pfaff
Sharon Rich

PROGRAM EDITOR
Kathleen Doyle

Ginn Publishing Canada Inc.

A Bear with Electric Hair
Anthology Level Three

© Copyright 1990 by
Ginn Publishing Canada Inc.
ALL RIGHTS RESERVED.

EDITORS
Sharon Stewart
Anne MacInnes

EDITORIAL CONSULTANT
Nicki Scrimger

ART/DESIGN
Sandi Meland Cherun/
Word & Image Design Studio

C99132
ISBN 0-7702-1702-8

Printed and bound in Canada.

EFGH 97654

Acknowledgments

For kind permission to reprint copyrighted material, acknowledgment is hereby made to the following:

Beatrice Schenk de Regniers for her poem "What's the Funniest Thing?" from *Something Special,* copyright © 1958, 1986 by Beatrice Schenk de Regniers. Published by Harcourt Brace & World, Inc. Reprinted by permission of the author.

David Higham Associates for "Conjuror" from *The Golden Unicorn* by Clive Sansom. Reprinted by permission of the publisher. Stoddart Publishing Co. Limited, Don Mills, for text and illustrations from *Moonbeam on a Cat's Ear* by Marie-Louise Gay. Reprinted by permission of the publisher.

Black Moss Press for "Albert's Bed," copyright © 1987. *Albert's Bed* by Herve Baudry was published by Black Moss Press, Windsor, Ontario, Canada, in 1987. Reprinted by permission of the publisher.

Shortland Publications Limited, Auckland, New Zealand, for excerpt from *The Gumby Shop.* Copyright © 1988 Shortland Publications Limited. Reprinted by permission of the publisher.

Ginn and Company Ltd. for *In My House* by Wes Magee, copyright © Ginn and Company Ltd. 1987. Originally published in England by Ginn and Company Ltd. Published in Canada/USA by Ginn and Company, Toronto, and The Wright Group, San Diego. Reprinted by permission of the publisher.

Greenwillow Books (A Division of William Morrow and Company, Inc.) for text only of excerpt from *Toby in the Country, Toby in the City* by Maxine Zohn Bozzo with illustrations by Frank Modell. Text copyright © 1982 by Maxine Zohn Bozzo. Reprinted by permission of Greenwillow Books (A Division of William Morrow and Company, Inc.)

Albert Whitman & Company for text only of excerpt from *Who Lives There?* by John Hawkinson, copyright © 1970 by Albert Whitman & Company. Reprinted by permission of the publisher.

Viking Penguin, a division of Penguin Books USA, Inc., for excerpt from *A House Is a House for Me* by Mary Ann Hoberman. Copyright © 1978 by Mary Ann Hoberman. All rights reserved. Reprinted by permission of Viking Penguin, a division of Penguin Books USA, Inc.

PHOTOGRAPHS:

Wolfgang Bayer/Bruce Coleman, 118 (inset photo); Daryl Benson/Masterfile, 121 (top); Ray Boudreau, 28-31; Canapress, 51 (bottom left and right); Bruce Coleman Inc., 120 (bottom); S.L. Craig, Jr./Bruce Coleman, 121 (bottom inset photo); Barbara Deans/Canapress, 52 (bottom left); Jack Dermid/Bruce Coleman, 118 (large photo); G.V. Faint/The Imago Bank, 51 (top inset photo); Peter D'Angelo/Focus Stock Photo, 52 (top left); Jeff Foott/Bruce Coleman, 119 (bottom); Benn Mitchell/The Image Bank, 50; John W. Mitchell/Bruce Coleman, 121 (bottom large photo); Nick Nicholson/The Image Bank, 51 (top large photo); John O'Brien, 52 (bottom right), 53; F. Patterson/Masterfile, 120 (top right); R.E. Pelham/Bruce Coleman, 120 (top left); L.L. Rue III/Bruce Coleman, 119 (top); See Spot Run, 32-36, 61-67, 92-94; Terry W. Self/Canapress, 52 (top right); Tony Thomas, 15-23; Harold Whyte, 95-98.

Every reasonable precaution has been taken to trace the owners of copyrighted material and to make due acknowledgment. Any omission will be gladly rectified in future editions.

Contents

On with the Show!	**6**

What's the Funniest Thing? 8
Poem   BEATRICE SCHENK DE REGNIERS

Knock-knock! 12
Jokes

The Little Red Hen 15
Play

Make a Puppet 24
"How-to" article

What Does It Take to Make a Clown? 28
Photo essay

Who Likes the Circus? 32
Article

Conjuror 37
Poem   CLIVE SANSOM

Where Are You Going? 40
Traditional rhyme

Moonbeam on a Cat's Ear 42
Picture-book story   MARIE-LOUISE GAY

Shadow Magic 50
Poem   ANNE MACINNES

Albert's Bed 54
Picture-book story   HERVE BAUDRY

The Gumby Shop 61
Poem excerpt   JOY COWLEY

Home Sweet Home 70

In My House 72
Poem WES MAGEE

In a Dark Wood 80
Traditional tale

Toby in the Country, 84
Toby in the City
Picture-book story MAXINE ZOHN BOZZO

The House that Jack Built 92
Traditional rhyme

Jack Builds a House 95
Article

The Three Little Pigs 99
Folk tale

Who Lives There? 108
Story JOHN HAWKINSON

A House Is a House 116
for Me
Poem excerpt MARY ANN HOBERMAN

Animal Homes 118
Photo essay ANNE MACINNES

Watch Out for Lions 122
Story CHRISTEL KLEITSCH

On with the Show!

— illustration of *Circus in the Wood* by Warabé Aska

What's the Funniest Thing?

by Beatrice Schenk de Regniers
Illustrated by Darcia LaBrosse

What's the funniest thing you can think of?
What's the funniest thing you can think of?

A monkey doing tricks?
A house built out of sticks?
An elephant juggling bricks?
What's the funniest thing *you* can think of?

What's the saddest thing you can think of?
What's the saddest thing you can think of?

To see a puppy cry?
Or a bird that cannot fly?
Or to have to say goodbye?
What's the saddest thing *you* can think of?

What's the noisiest thing you can think of?
What's the noisiest thing you can think of?

One hundred birds chirping?
A great giant burping?
Ten soup slurpers slurping?
What's the noisiest thing *you* can think of?

What's the quietest thing you can think of?
What's the quietest thing you can think of?

Grass growing?
Snow snowing?
A soft breeze blowing?
What's the quietest thing *you* can think of?

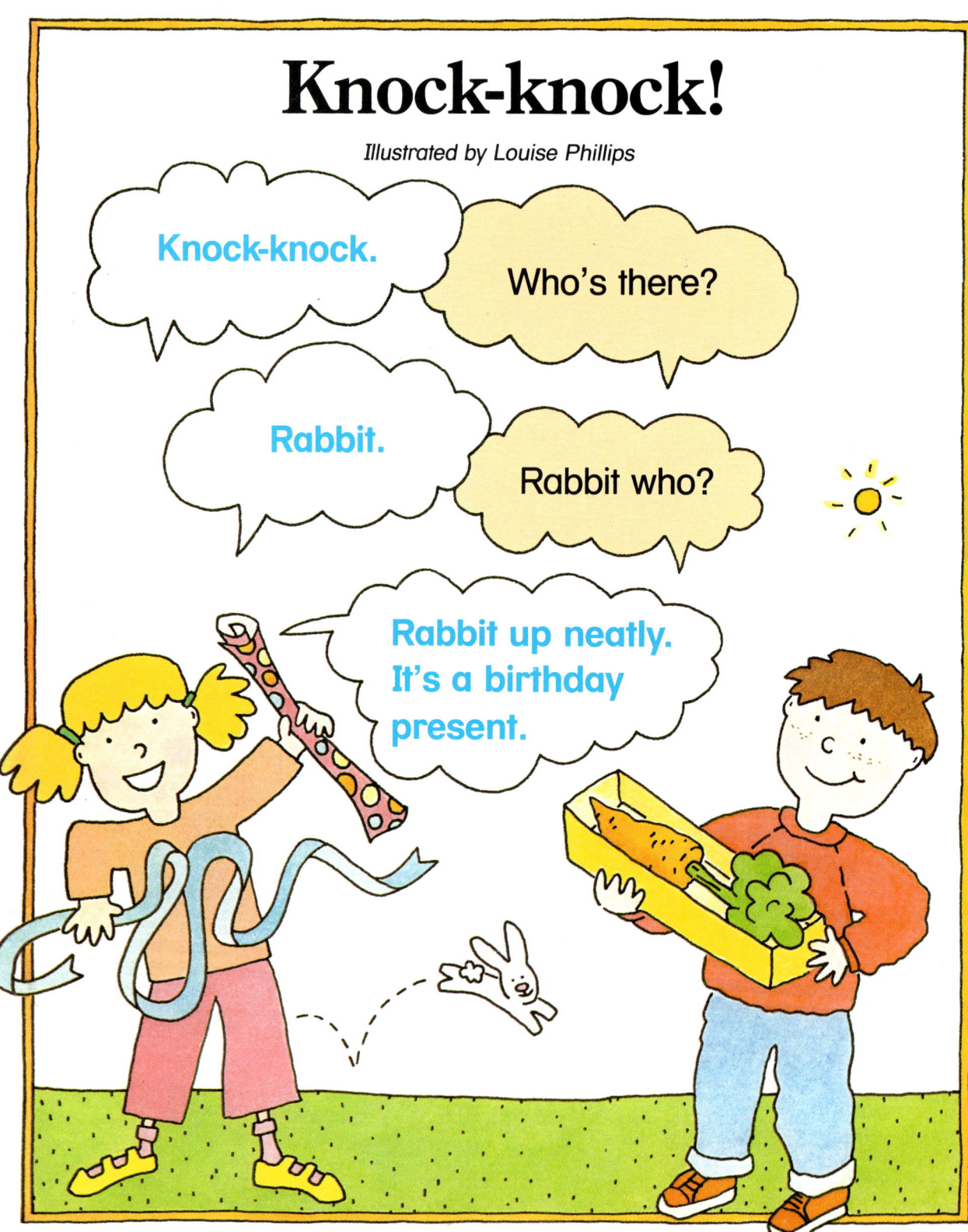

The Little Red Hen

Photographed by Tony Thomas

Puppets and sets by Laurie Stein

LITTLE RED HEN: Look what I found! I'll plant this grain of wheat and make some good bread.
Who will help me?

CAT: Meow, meow, not I!
DOG: Ruff, ruff, not I!
PIG: Oink, oink, not I!
LITTLE RED HEN: Cluck, cluck, then I'll do it by myself.
NARRATOR: And she did.

And she did.

LITTLE RED HEN: Now it's time to cut the ripe wheat. Who will help me?

CAT: Meow, meow, not I!

DOG: Ruff, ruff, not I!

PIG: Oink, oink, not I!

LITTLE RED HEN: Cluck, cluck, then I'll do it by myself.

NARRATOR: And she did.

LITTLE RED HEN: Now it's time to take the wheat to the mill and grind it into flour. Who will help me?

CAT: Meow, meow, not I!

DOG: Ruff, ruff, not I!

PIG: Oink, oink, not I!

LITTLE RED HEN: Cluck, cluck, then I'll do it by myself.

NARRATOR: And she did.

LITTLE RED HEN: Now it's time to make this flour into bread dough.
Who will help me?

CAT: Meow, meow, not I!

DOG: Ruff, ruff, not I!

PIG: Oink, oink, not I!

LITTLE RED HEN: Cluck, cluck, then I'll do it by myself.

NARRATOR: And she did.

LITTLE RED HEN: Now it's time to bake the bread. Who will help me?

CAT: Meow, meow, not I!

DOG: Ruff, ruff, not I!

PIG: Oink, oink, not I!

LITTLE RED HEN: Cluck, cluck, then I'll do it by myself.

NARRATOR: And she did.

LITTLE RED HEN: Now it's time to eat the bread. Who will help me?
CAT: Meow, meow, I will!
DOG: Ruff, ruff, I will!
PIG: Oink, oink, I will!

LITTLE RED HEN: Cluck, cluck, no you won't!
I found the grain of wheat,
I planted the seed,
I cut the ripe wheat,
I took the wheat to the mill,

I made the flour into bread dough,
I baked the loaf of bread,
all by myself.
So I shall **eat** the bread
all by myself!

NARRATOR: And that is just what she did.

Make a Puppet

Illustrated by Linda Hendry

Stick Puppet

What you need:
paper in different colors
scissors
crayons or paint
glue or tape
stick

What you do:

Draw an animal on a piece of paper.

Cut out the animal.

Glue or tape it on a stick.

Put on a show with your puppets.

Paper Bag Puppet

What you need:
paper bag
crayons or paint
scissors
yarn or string
glue or tape

What you do:

Draw a face on a paper bag.

Glue or tape on some hair.

Put your hand in the bag.

Put on a show with your puppets.

What Does It Take

Photographed by

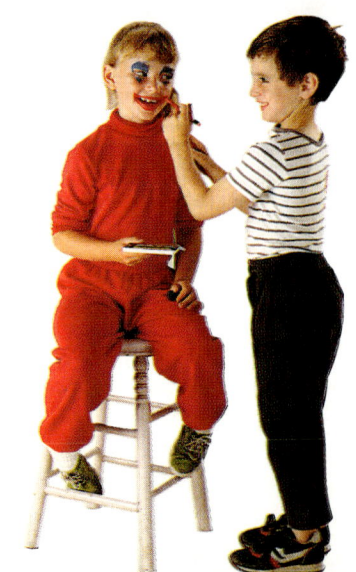

It takes a funny face—
white make-up,
blue eyebrows,
a red mouth,
and a big, round, shiny nose.

to Make a Clown?

Ray Boudreau

It takes a funny wig—
purple, blue, white,
and frizzy.

It takes a funny costume—
straw hat, neck-tie skirt,
white gloves,
and pom-pom shoes.

It takes funny tricks—
slipping on a banana peel,
squirting water from a flower,
twirling an umbrella
and walking a tightrope—
on the ground!

Who Likes the Circus?

Illustrated by Laurie Stein

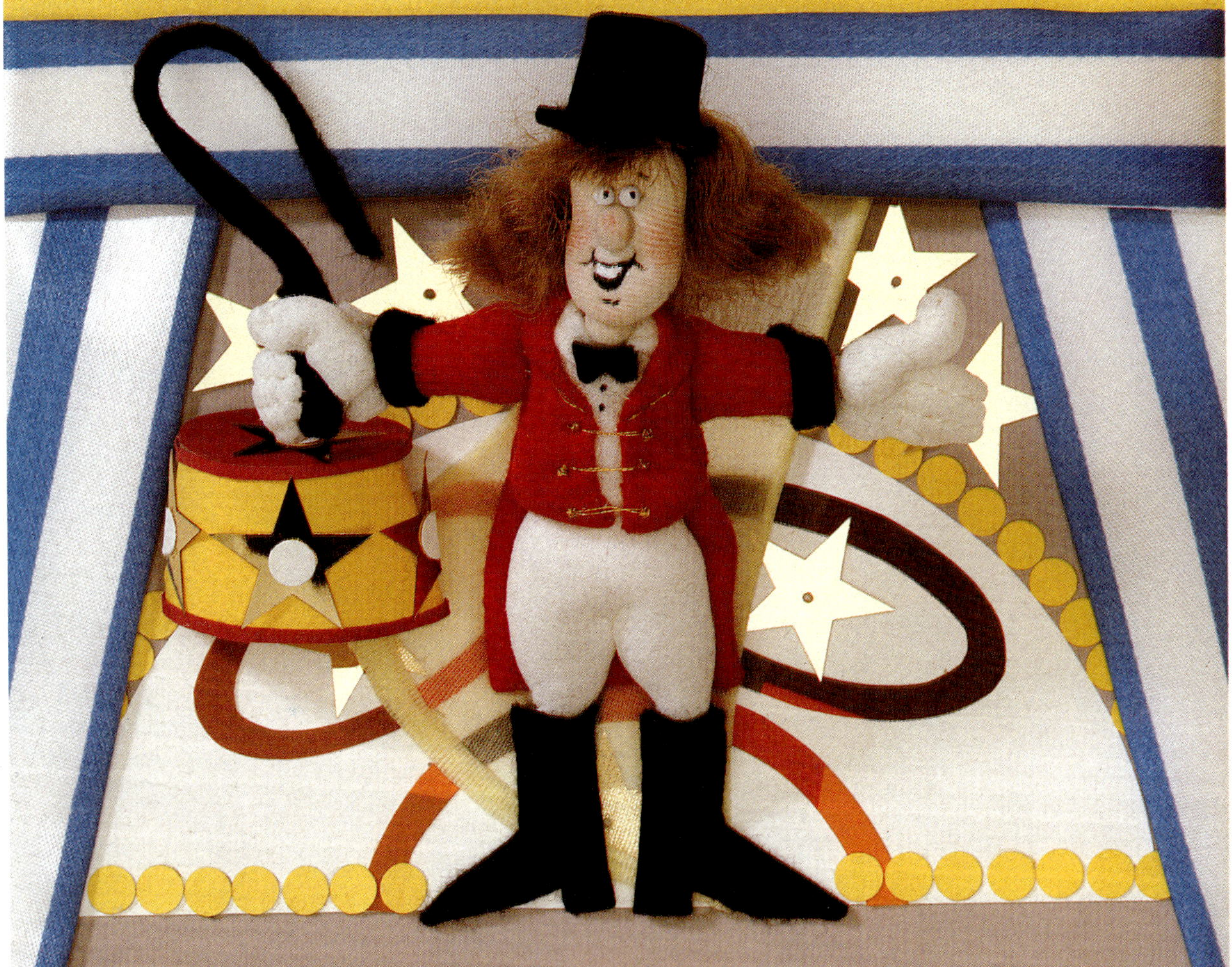

I do! I start the show off and keep the acts moving in the three rings.
I'm the **ringmaster.**

Photographed by See Spot Run

I do! I toss balls and bowling pins into the air and catch them before they fall.
I'm the **juggler.**

We do! We swing from a trapeze and walk a tightrope high above the ground. We're the acrobats.

We do! We slip on banana peels and trip over our shoes and play silly tricks.
We're the **clowns.**

We do! We clap and cheer and gasp and laugh.
We're the **audience.**

Conjuror

by Clive Sansom
Illustrated by Kelly Jobson

He takes an empty hat—
Like that—
Raps it . . . taps it . . .
And out pops a rabbit in a large pink bow!
    How does he do it?
    How **does** he do it?
    How does he **do** it?
    I would like to know.

He takes an old stick—
Just a trick—
Raps it . . . taps it . . .
And there's a string of colored flags all in a row!
    How does he do it?
    How **does** he do it?
    How does he **do** it?
    I would like to know.

He takes a small book—
Now look!
Raps it . . . taps it . . .
Changes it to turtledoves and lets them all go!
    How does he do it?
    How **does** he do it?
    How does he **do** it?
    I would like to know.

Where Are You Going?

Illustrated by Thach Bui

Where are you going
You little pig?
I'm going to town
To get me a wig.

A wig, little pig?
A pig in a wig?
Who ever before saw
A pig in a wig!

Where are you going
You little cat?
I'm going to town
To get me a hat.

A hat, little cat?
A cat in a hat?
Who ever before saw
A cat in a hat!

Moonbeam on a Cat's Ear

Written and illustrated by Marie-Louise Gay

A new moon
shining on a cat's ear.
The cat is dreaming
that a mouse is near.

Knock, knock, knock!
Who's there?

It's Toby Toby
with the bright red hair.

Come on, Rosie!
Come out with me!

Let's play in the shadow
of the apple tree.

Now, if I climb real high,
I can pull the moon
right out of the sky.

Shall we sail to Rio, or fly to Mars,

or wander through
the clouds and stars?

Was it a dream
or did they really try
to steal the moon
right out of the sky?

Shadow Magic
by Anne MacInnes

Shadows fall
on ground
and wall,

Some are **BIG** . . . .

and some are small.

Shadows cool the summer heat

On sandy beach . . . .

and city street.

51

Shadows shrink

and

s t r e t c h

and c l i m b;

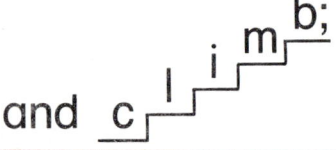

Shadows even tell
the time.

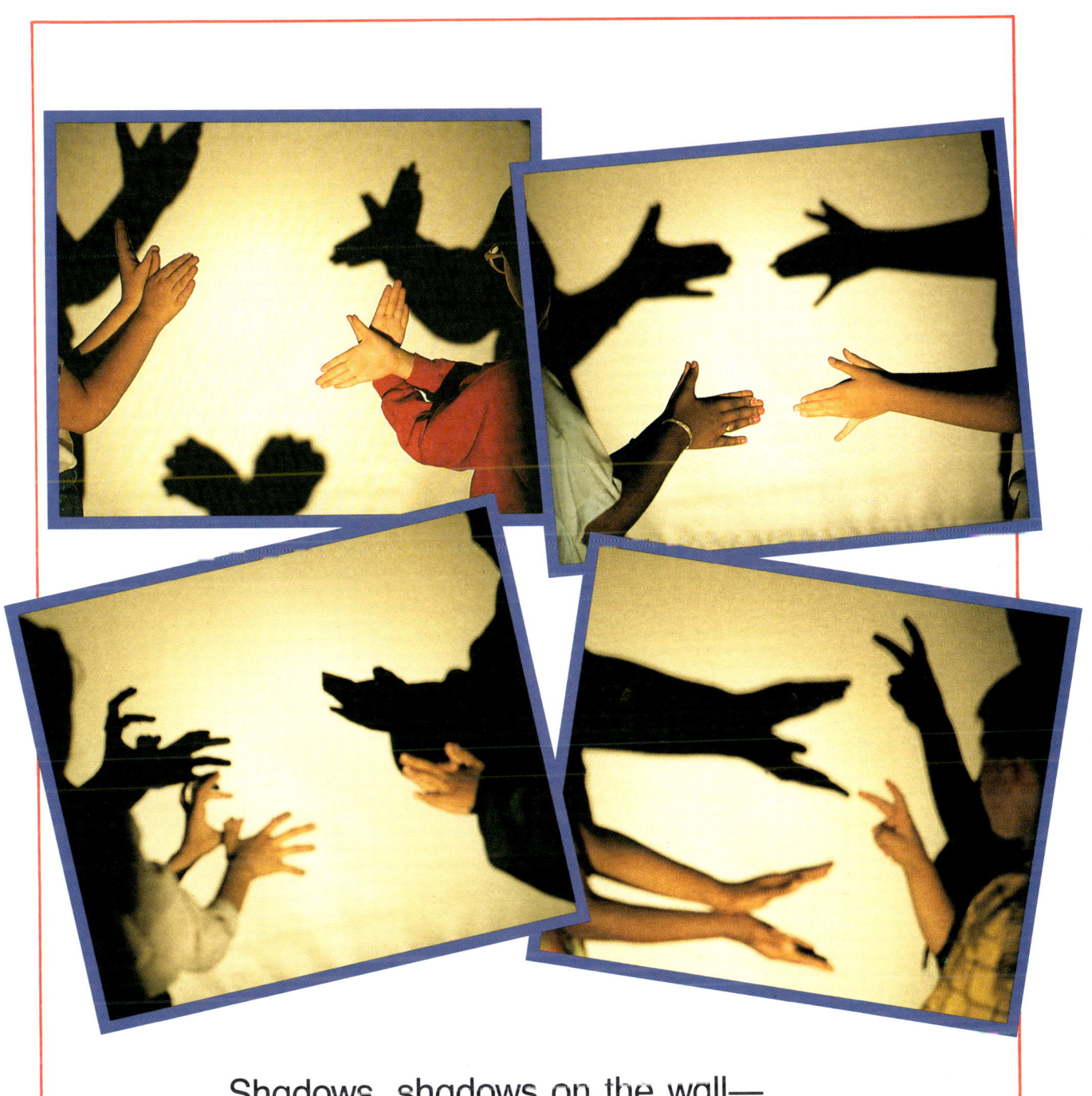

Shadows, shadows on the wall—
Which animal do you like best of all?

Albert's Bed

Written and illustrated by Herve Baudry

Albert is ill.
His doctor said that
he must stay in bed today,
but what can Albert do?

Albert imagines that his bed is a boat . . .

a plane . . .

a circus act . . .

a boxing ring . . .

He could be an explorer . . .
at the North Pole . . .

or in Africa . . .

or he could be a race-car driver . . .

or a famous goalie . . .

or a deep-sea diver . . .

Albert imagines that his bed bridges the greatest canyons . . .

or that it is a great seesaw . . .

But,
the doctor did say that Albert should rest, didn't he?

The Gumby Shop

by Joy Cowley
Illustrated by Jackie Snider

Let's stop at the Gumby shop.

What shall we buy?

Some cheese, some cheese from bumblebees.

You can't buy cheese from bumblebees.

You can at the Gumby shop.

Let's stop at the Gumby shop.

What shall we buy?

Some meat, some meat to wear on your feet.

You can't buy meat to wear on your feet.

You can at the Gumby shop.

Let's stop at the Gumby shop.

What shall we buy?

A bed, a bed
made out of bread.

You can't buy a bed
made out of bread.

You can at the Gumby shop.

Let's stop at the Gumby shop.

What shall we buy?

A bear, a bear
with electric hair.

You can't buy a bear
with electric hair.

You can at the Gumby shop.

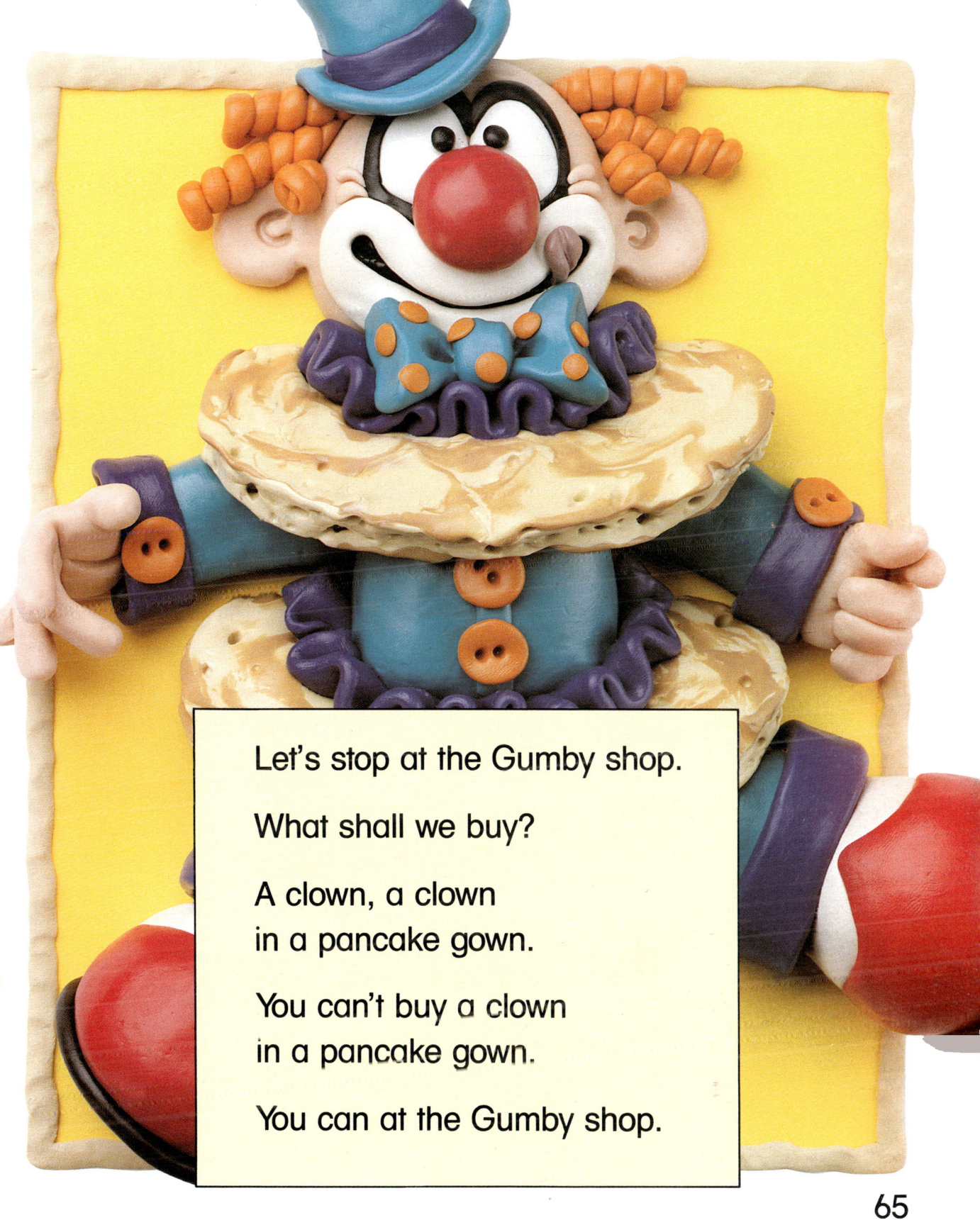

Let's stop at the Gumby shop.

What shall we buy?

A clown, a clown
in a pancake gown.

You can't buy a clown
in a pancake gown.

You can at the Gumby shop.

Let's stop at the Gumby shop.

What shall we buy?

Some eggs, some eggs with purple legs.

You can't buy eggs with purple legs.

You can at the Gumby shop.

Let's stop at the Gumby shop.

What shall we buy?

Some jeans, some jeans to fit sardines.

You can't buy jeans to fit sardines.

You can at the Gumby shop.

Let's stop at the Gumby shop.

What shall we buy?

A snail, a snail
with a rose on its tail.

You can't buy a snail
with a rose on its tail.

You can at the Gumby shop.

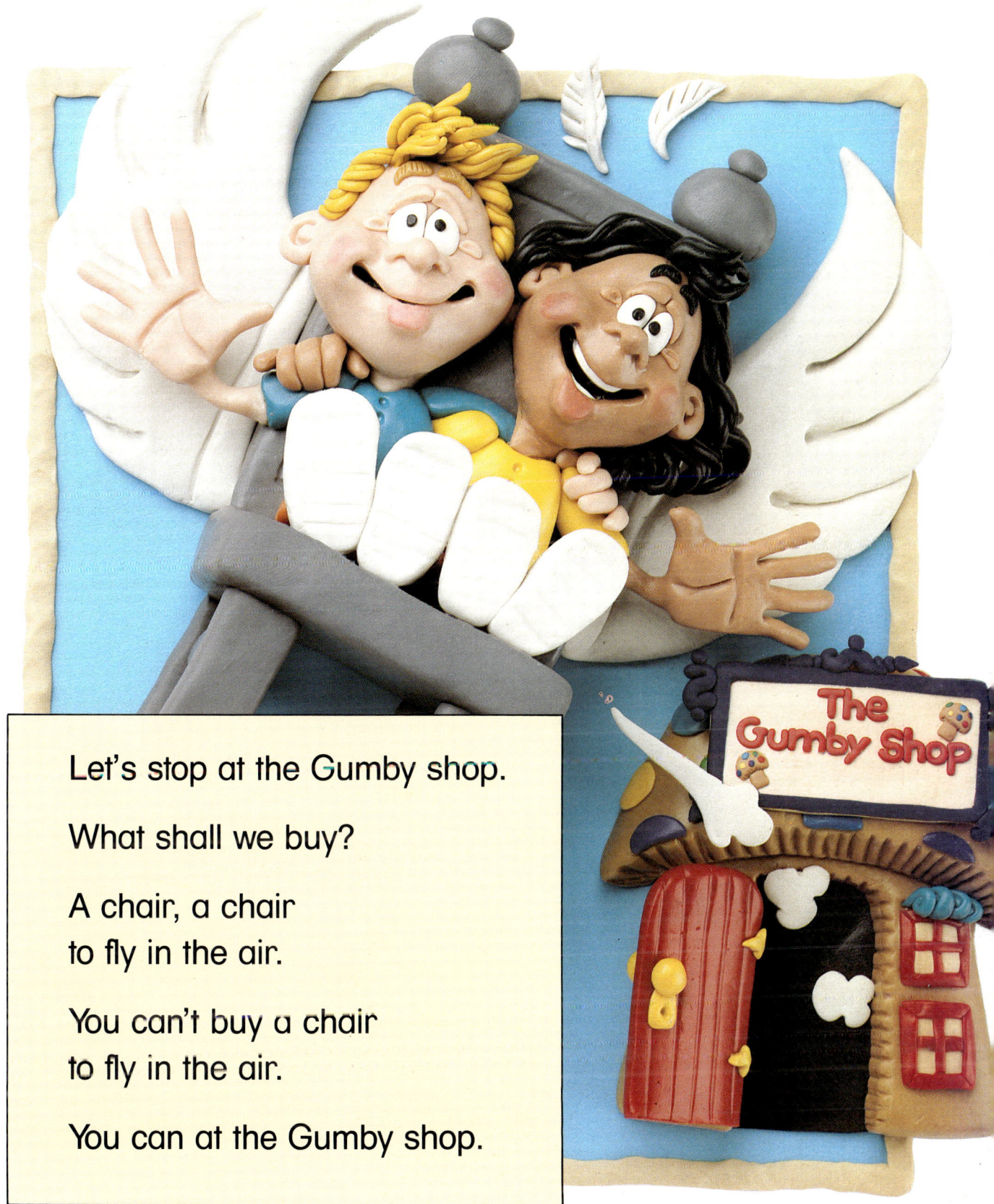

Let's stop at the Gumby shop.

What shall we buy?

A chair, a chair
to fly in the air.

You can't buy a chair
to fly in the air.

You can at the Gumby shop.

Home Sweet Home

— from *Have You Seen Josephine?*, written and illustrated by Stéphane Poulin

In My House

by Wes Magee
Illustrated by Joanne Fitzgerald

In the hall
a fat spider
is slowly,
slowly spinning a web.

It's dark,
oh so dark
in the hall.

In the kitchen
my black cat
is sleeping,
sleeping on a chair.

It's warm,
oh so warm
in the kitchen.

In the front room
my sister
is dancing,
dancing to her pop music.

It's noisy,
oh so noisy
in the front room.

In the bathroom
a silver tap
is dripping,
dripping.
Plink!   Plink!   Plonk!

It's cold,
oh so cold
in the bathroom.

In the attic
a brown mouse
is running,
running in the dark.

It's creepy,
oh so creepy
in the attic.

In my bedroom
the animals
are standing,
standing in a line.

It's safe,
oh so safe
in my bedroom.

In my house
there are lots of places,
lots of secret places.
I watch
and I listen
and nobody knows
I am there.

Nobody knows I am there.

In a Dark Wood

Illustrated by Jirina Marton

In a dark, dark wood,
there was a dark, dark house,

And in that dark, dark house,
there was a dark, dark room,

And in that dark, dark room, there was a dark, dark cupboard,

And in that dark, dark cupboard, there was a dark, dark shelf,

And on that dark, dark shelf, there was a dark, dark box,

And in that dark, dark box, there was a

Toby in the Country, Toby in the City

by Maxine Zohn Bozzo
Illustrated by Daniel Sylvestre

I live in the country,
and my name is Toby.

I live in the city,
and my name is Toby.

My house looks like this.

My house looks like this.

My street looks like this, and has trees.

My street looks like this, and has trees.

After school I like to play with my friends.

After school I like to play with my friends.

Sometimes it's winter in the country . . .
and I like to play in the snow.

Sometimes it's winter in the city . . .
and I like to play in the snow.

When it is spring in the country . . .
I see lots of flowers.

When it is spring in the city . . .
I see lots of flowers.

When summer comes to the country . . .
I like to go to the beach.

When summer comes to the city . . .
I like to go to the beach.

I like to visit the country.

I like to visit the city.

Illustrated by
Phyllis Wong Kun

This is the house
that Jack built.

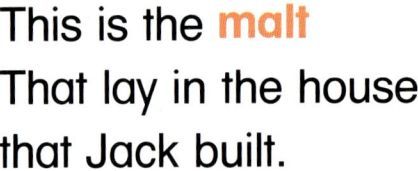

This is the **malt**
That lay in the house
that Jack built.

This is the **rat,**
That ate the malt
That lay in the house
that Jack built.

This is the **cat,**
That killed the rat,
That ate the malt
That lay in the house
that Jack built.

This is the **dog,**
That worried the cat,
That killed the rat,
That ate the malt
That lay in the house
that Jack built.

This is the **cow** with the crumpled horn,
That tossed the dog,
That worried the cat,
That killed the rat,
That ate the malt
That lay in the house
that Jack built.

Jack Builds a House

Adapted from the nursery rhyme *Photographed by Harold Whyte*

This is the house that Jack built.

This is the basement
that's under the house that Jack built.
This is the floor over the basement
that's under the house that Jack built.

Here are the walls
that stand on the floor
over the basement
that's under the house that Jack built.

This is the roof
that sits on the walls
that stand on the floor
over the basement
that's under the house that Jack built.

The Three Little Pigs

Illustrated by Vesna Krstanovitch

Once upon a time, there were three little pigs who lived with their mother. One day the mother pig said, "You are old enough now to live on your own." So the three little pigs set off to build their own houses.

The first little pig met a man with some straw. The pig said, "I want to build a house. Sell me your straw." The man did, and the first little pig built a house of straw.

The second little pig met a man with some sticks. The pig said, "I want to build a house. Sell me your sticks." The man did, and the second little pig built a house of sticks.

The third little pig met a man with some bricks. The pig said, "I want to build a house. Sell me your bricks." The man did, and the third little pig built a house of bricks.

One day a big bad wolf came along to the straw house. "Little pig, little pig, let me come in," he said.

"No, no," cried the first little pig. "Not by the hair of my chinny chin chin."

"Then I'll huff and I'll puff and I'll blow your house in," said the big bad wolf.

So he huffed and he puffed and he blew the house in. The first little pig ran over to the stick house.

The big bad wolf went along to the stick house. "Little pig, little pig, let me come in," he said.

"No, no," cried the second little pig. "Not by the hair of my chinny chin chin."

"Then I'll huff and I'll puff and I'll blow your house in," said the big bad wolf.

So he huffed and he puffed and he blew the house in. The first little pig and the second little pig ran over to the brick house.

The big bad wolf went along to the brick house. "Little pig, little pig, let me come in," he said.

"No, no," cried the third little pig. "Not by the hair of my chinny chin chin."

"Then I'll huff and I'll puff and I'll blow your house in," said the big bad wolf.

So he huffed and he puffed, and he puffed and he huffed, but he could not blow the house in.

"Then I'll come down your chimney!" shouted the big bad wolf.

"Quick, let's put a pot of hot water under the chimney!" cried the third little pig.

The three little pigs got the pot and put it under the chimney, and just in time!

The wolf came down the chimney and—**splash**—fell into the pot of hot water.

"Yowww!" yelled the big bad wolf. He jumped out of the pot, ran out of the door, and was never seen again. And the three little pigs lived together happily ever after.

Who Lives There?

by John Hawkinson
Illustrated by Bo Kim Louie

One fine day as I walked down a country road, I saw a tree with a hole in the trunk.

I wonder—who lives there?

Little flying squirrels sleeping until sundown?

Or a mother screech owl with two fuzzy owlets?

Way up high in a tall pine tree I saw a nest of sticks.

I wonder—who lives up there?

Could be an eagle, with little white eaglets,

or maybe one sleepy old crow.

Down in the meadow I found a hollow log.

I wonder—who lives in there?

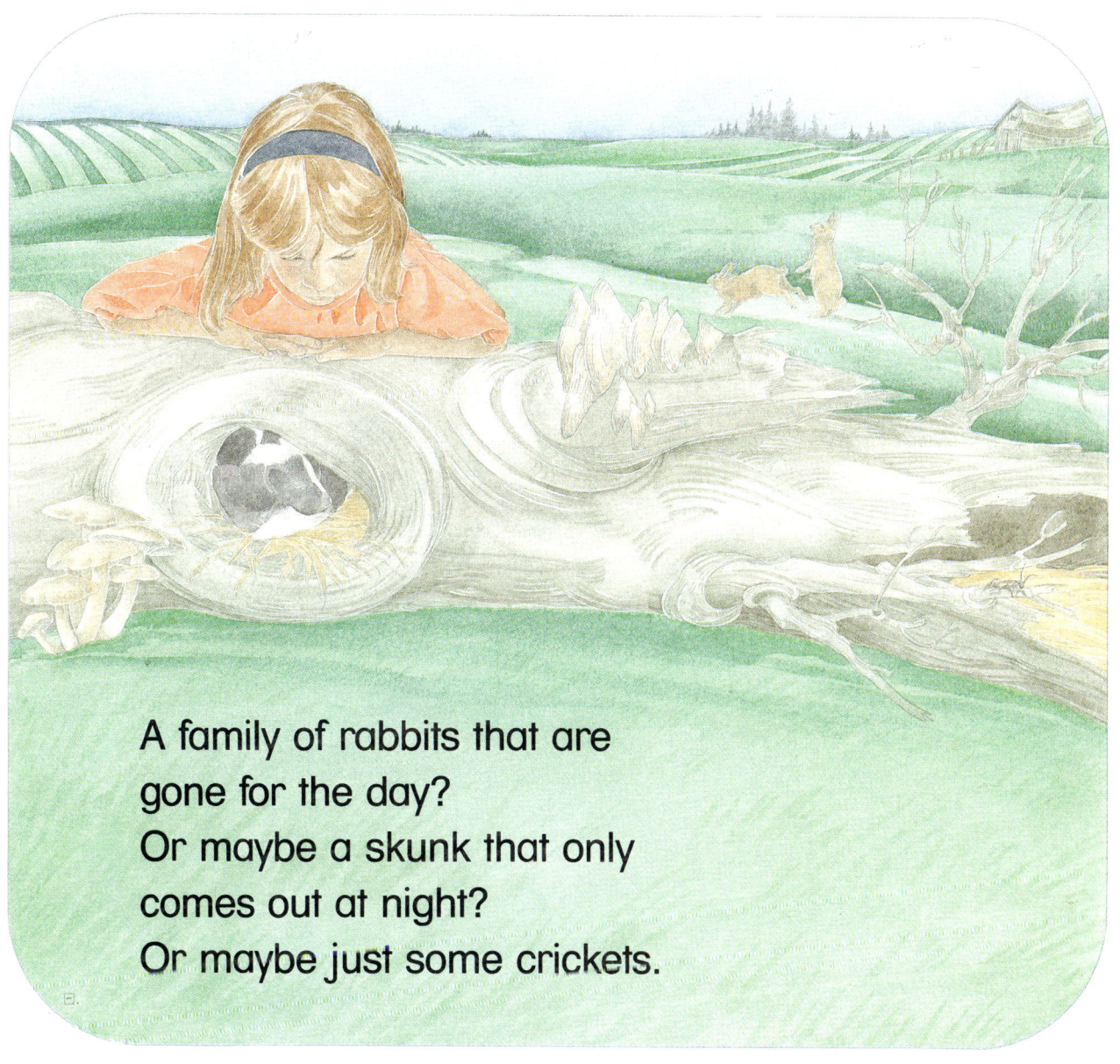

A family of rabbits that are gone for the day?
Or maybe a skunk that only comes out at night?
Or maybe just some crickets.

I saw an old barn with the roof caved in.

I wonder—who lives in there?

Barn swallows
or barn owls,
or rats
and bats
that like the
dark?

On my way home, I saw a small hole
in an old apple tree.

I looked in the hole
and I didn't see a thing.

I listened at the hole
and didn't hear a thing.

I put my finger in the hole
and didn't feel a thing.

Then I put my mouth to the hole and
whispered, "Does anyone live in there?"

And do you know what?

A little brown mouse
peeked out of that hole,
and
>I think
>>he smiled at me!

A House Is a House for Me

by Mary Ann Hoberman
Illustrated by Eugenie Fernandes

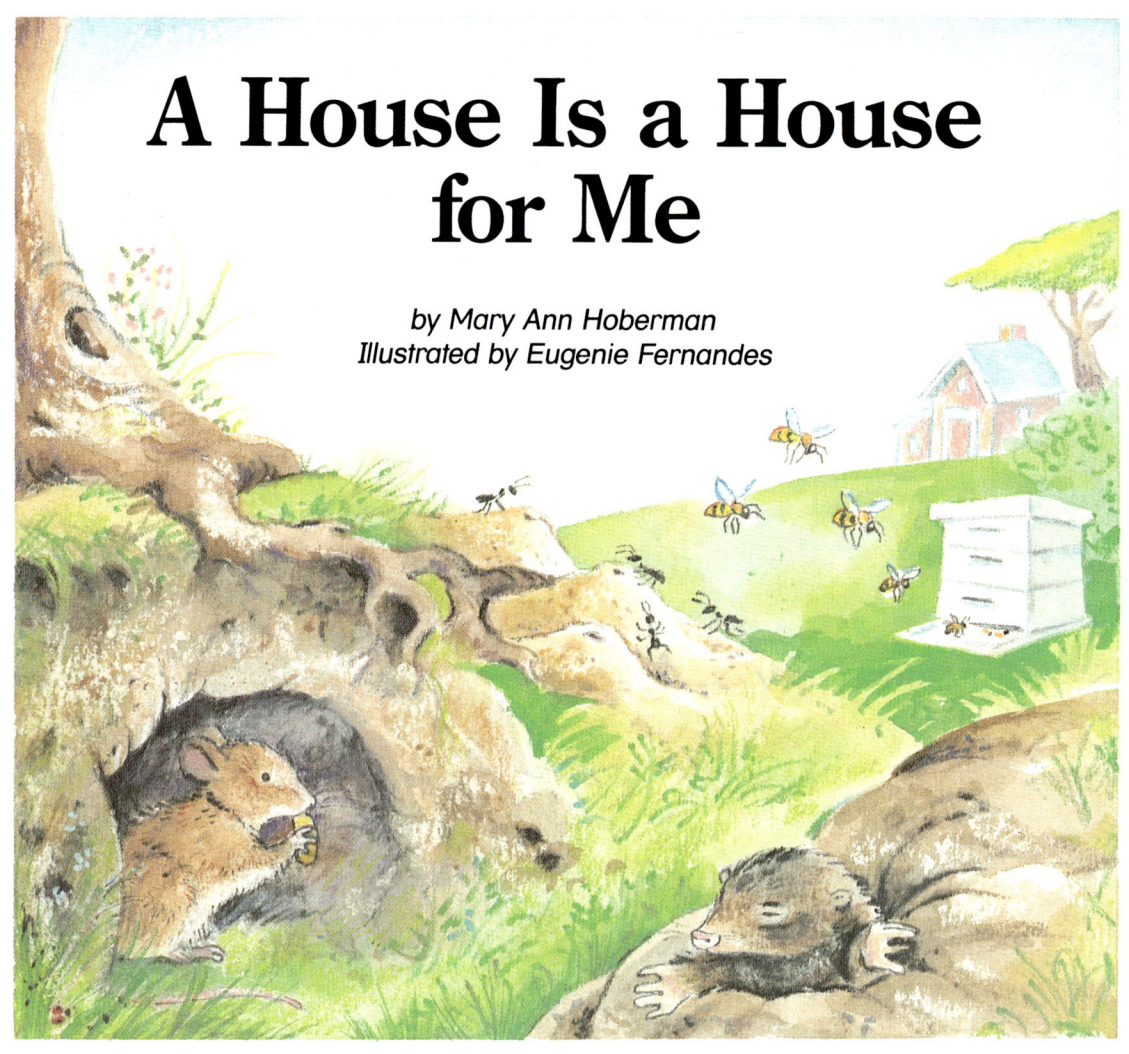

A hill is a house for an ant, an ant.
A hive is a house for a bee.
A hole is a house for a mole or a mouse
And a house is a house for me!

A web is a house for a spider.
A bird builds its nest in a tree.

There is nothing so snug as a bug in a rug
And a house is a house for me!

Animal Homes

by Anne MacInnes

Beavers live in **lodges** made out of mud, stones, and sticks. A beaver lodge has a big room above the water, but the ways into the home are under the water.

Foxes live in **dens.** They make their dens in hollow logs or trees, or among large rocks.

Birds live in **nests.** They build their nests out of mud, grass, twigs, and anything they find that will make a nest.

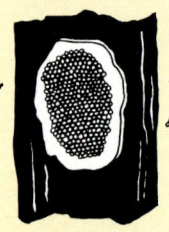 Bees live in **hives.** They make their hives in hollow trees. Sometimes they make their homes in boxes that people make.

 Chipmunks live in **burrows** under the ground. They store grain, nuts, and seeds in their burrows to eat during the winter.

Spiders live in **webs.** The sticky webs catch bugs for the spiders to eat.

Ants live in **anthills.** They dig long, long tunnels under the ground with a room at the end of each tunnel.

Watch Out for Lions

by Christel Kleitsch
Illustrated by Mike Martchenko

It was a rainy day.
"We can't go out to play," said Jake. "I don't like to stay inside. What can we do in here?"

"Let's make a playhouse," said Tessa. "Here's a big chair. Let's put the two little chairs beside it. Help me put blankets over the chairs."

"Now we have a tent," said Jake. "Watch out for snakes and watch out for lions."

"Jake, I can see a lion now," said Tessa. "Get in the tent."

Tessa and Jake hid in the tent.

"Sh," said Jake, "sh."

They waited and waited for the lion to go away.

"Has the lion gone yet?" asked Jake.

"I'll go out and look," said Tessa.

She looked out of the tent. "I don't see him," she said. "I think he's gone."
But the lion had **not** gone.

Down he jumped.
Down went the blankets.
Down went the tent.
Meow!

"What a funny lion," said Tessa.

Illustrations used in unit openers:

Illustration of *Circus in the Wood* by Warabé Aska. Copyright © 1989 Warabé Aska.

Illustration from *Have You Seen Josephine?* by Stéphane Poulin, copyright © 1986 by Stéphane Poulin, reprinted by permission of Tundra Books.